Of Time and Small Islands

A Canarian Sequence

by

Walter Nash

Introduction

Of Time and Small Islands first appeared in 2004 as an online text, published in Arizona by Gary David of Island Hill Books. I owe him many thanks for his encouragement. For the production of this printed version I am greatly indebted to Hugh Hellicar, who has exercised his editorial skill and tact in a sensitive and perceptive arrangement of the poems.

Mr Hellicar reminds me that I have by now known the islands in several perspectives: at first as a tourist, then as a regular visitor over longer periods, and finally as a permanent resident. These differing standpoints have implied some variations of style: the poems are postcards, are travelogues, are diaries, are reports, are histories, are social commentaries or political reflections.

Whatever the style, may I hope that they will express my love for all that is good in the islands, my concern for all that is under threat, and a sense of fellowship with the unknown reader, my companion, who may be prompted to visit the Hesperides with camera and pencil, and make better notes on the spirit of the place.

Walter Nash

FOREWORD

This sequence of verse in an easy lilt captures the charm of **The Canary Islands**. Written with a fond eye by a seasoned resident of **Tenerife**, these pages invite the traveller into a fascination for the history behind the vibrant local life.

Walter Nash was Professor of English Language at Nottingham University, and continues to write in retirement. The leisurely musing in these poems are a reminder of the *holiday vision* open to all, and the stimulus of travel. The quest for meaning and the outlook of Faith are parts of the gentle purpose moving the rhythm of words along.

These narrative lines make writing seem easy, and musing a creative use of time. At the least they should encourage you to keep a diary on holiday.

To me this book is also a valuable reminder of how versatile the English language is, at its best.

Hugh Hellicar
Publisher

Published by Beyond the Cloister Publications
Brighton BN2 1FH England

Copyright: Walter Nash 2006

No part of this publication may be reproduced, stored in a retrieved system, or transmitted in any form, or by any means, electronic, mechanical, photocopying, recording or otherwise, without the permission of the author.

ISBN 1-899605-118
978-1-899605-118

Printed and bound by CPI Antony Rowe, Eastbourne

By the same author:

Rhetoric—the Wit of Persuasion
Blackwells 1989

An Uncommon Language
Routledge 1992

Language and Creative Illusion
Longmans 1999

The Spirit Soars
Feather Books 1999

A Departed Music
Anglo-Saxon Books 2006

Pilgrimages (Co-Editor)
Feather Books 2006

Beyond the Cloister Publications

14 Lewes Crescent Brighton BN2 1FH
England
beyondcloister@hotmail.co.uk

Contents

Of Time and Small Islands	8
Poem: *Of Time and Small Islands*	9
The Coast of the Giants	10
Poem: *A Moment by the Acantilado de Los Gigantes*	10
Lanzarote	13
Poem: *Three Tinted Views of Lanzarote*	
Poem: *The Fire Mountains*	16
Tenerife	
Poem: *A Fallen Empire*	18
Poem: *Tenerife*	20
El Hierro	
Poem: *Landing Hard*	22
Poem: *El Golfo*	24
Poem: *Isla de Tranquilidad*	25
Poem: *Las Montañetas*	26
Poem: *Hoya del Morcillo*	27
Poem: *La Restinga*	28
Poem: *Mirador de Isora*	
Flower Pieces	
Poem: *A Career Model*	32
Poem: *The Bonniest Bush*	33
Poem: *The Bougainvillea Lunch*	34

Poem: *Incomers 2000 AD*	38
Fuerteventura	41
Poem: *Fuerteventura*	41
The Eighth Island	44
Poem: *The Eighth Island*	44
Poem: *Colophon*	46
The Skies	47
Poem: *Weather Wisdoms*	47
Poem: *Easter in the Pueblo*	51
Poem: *Epiphany in the Pueblo*	53
The Patroness of Tenerife	
Poem: *Nuestra Señora de Las Nieves*	57
New Year	
Poem: *Another New Year*	59
Canarian Hours	61
Poem: *Canarian Hours*	
Poem: *Mañana*	63
Poem: *Entre Chien et Loup*	64
Poem: *Morena Salada*	65
Poem: *A Nocturne for Atlantis*	
Have to Leave	71

Of Time and Small Islands

An archipelago of volcanoes: beyond Carthage, beyond the Gates of Hercules, lying off Moorish Africa in the huge, truculent sea that flows away to *finis*. The ancients called them the Hesperides, or else the Fortunate Isles or the Islands of the Blest. Some believed them to be the Elysian Fields, reserved for the ease of Homeric heroes. They can be reached *in four hours from London, on daily flights*.

They are part of the geological structure of Macaronesia, which reaches down from the Azores and Madeira to a southerly terminus in the Islands of Cape Verde. They rose out of the tumult of the undersea millions of years ago, and now in affrighted tranquillity await their regression.

These are the Isles of Canary, *Canaria* being the name given to one of them by Pliny the Elder (on account of its hearsay number of large dogs). Canary is many things.

> Canary is a climate of microclimates
> Canary is a pleasant cauldron of winds
> Canary is a flowery heaven,
>   immensely fruitful among its unyielding barrenness
> Canary is the almond tree escaped into the hills,
>   the hibiscus and oleander corralled in the town gardens
> Canary is the fiesta
> Canary is the lava field
>   the detritus of catastrophic eruptions
> Canary is the breeze-block rubble,
>   the golf resort, the brash, flash hotel.
>
> People come to Canary with their hopes
>   and sometimes their expectations are fulfilled.

Canary is a history of war, slavery,
          toil, catastrophe, commerce.
Canary shows where history brings us
          and is prophetic of our fall.
Canary is for some a quest.
Canary is a haunting, an apparition, a spirit of place.

Proem

Of time and these small islands runs the tale,
time fossicking around the fire-born rock
that crumples to the tide's incessant shock;
against that beat, basalt itself is frail.

It will take time to undermine the bluff
before the tide invades the lava-flows
and tilts the hills into the sea. Who knows,
another thousand years ? Still time enough

for human enterprise to have its say.
Conquest and viticulture come to pass,
fisheries and bananas, then the crass
casinos in white concrete. Though one day

the ocean will lose patience, mountains crack
and spill their smelting on the beach, yet still
the headlands hold the course of heaven's will.
For these small islands, there's no turning back.

The Coast of the Giants

The eastern islands of Lanzarote and Fuerteventura are low-profiled, and at sea level descend into expanses of white sand. Other islands have the conical or coolie-hatted profile characterising a central volcanic upthrust. They swoop to the sea down steep ravines —*barrancos*— which terminate in blacksand beaches and huge cliffs. Such a cliffwall is called an *acantilado*. The ten-mile-long coastal cliff in the north-western corner of Tenerife is called the *Acantilado de los Gigantes*, the 'Coast of the Giants'. The *Acantilado* rises vertically some fifteen hundred feet above sea level. It is commandingly impressive. And the cliffs are not black, as the guide books say; they change colour hour by hour, light by light. You cannot gaze at them for long without being abstracted into reverie.

A Moment by the Acantilado de Los Gigantes

Muss es sein ? Es muss sein !
(epigraph in the final movement of Beethoven's last quartet)

*A thousand feet high and reaching massively south
from Teno light to the spruce margin of a tourist haven
ten miles away, a crinkled buttress of basalt braves
onslaught of seas that unremittingly strike and seethe.
This is the Acantilado. Wandering fingers of light
fondle its riven face as the sun works round the day,
defining its ropes of rock, its clefts and courses and cavelets,
never two hours the same, yet changeless early and late.*

*It is worth more than a photograph from the deck of a boat
that brings its passengers to view the dolphins or take a dip
in the bay of Masca; it merits more than a word from
                              the trippers
at lunch by the pool, who ignore the sea's incessant beat.
This is an image of time and beyond time, a sign
capturing aeons complete in the lens of a round minute
out of the ceaseless tremor of earth's primeval skin;
a moment of the eternal in this noonday's singular scene.*

*Out in the sound, a fisherman in his blue-gunwaled skiff
is tending his flimsy nets, making a wayward killing
on a trading floor where current trends never hold still;
one error, and the mocking breakers clap and scoff;
wise, when the storm wind prompts, out of the pallid west,
he'll run for Teno's bleak beach, or sothward a mile
to Santiago, where the indispensable Virgin sits smiling
in her hut on the harbour wall, shelter from the ocean's worst.*

*And if I envy him it is not in some fey, addled belief
that a life of endangered toil is the virtuous life. No.
Nor will I put his decent human pretensions lower
than anyone else's to goods and ease and consoling love;
but still I think the soul of him less able to come to harm
as long as his hunch'd and weather'd hopes remain thus oddly
poised between the stark Atlantic and the simple mother of
                              God.
A free man ? Free. And sentenced. In prison, at home.*

*Suddenly the gull soars, snowy-vanned, her broad
span sketching a Christ-cross on the virginal blue;
image of the soul's flight; nothing of earth pursuing,
she turns and pauses at heaven's porch like an entering bride;*
es muss sein *! And I proclaim the soul's existence, proclaim
against my unbelief, against the coming dark; cry
how the spirit soars up again and again, flying
in the face of chaos, reaching for glory in the long climb.*

*Cry against the dark. Where the dragon-tailed rollers writhe,
cry. We are not made to eat, drink and fester
in black earth; clogged in the worst, cry for the best,
then disgrace shows a semblance of honour, an also-runner's*
                                                                wreath.
*But see —the anguished second passes, the mountains stand,
their doomsday grandeur ingrained in their still impassive*
                                                                features,
*and green-coiled, spurning serpents roll to the beach
and welter and hiss and die in the black volcanic sand.*

Lanzarote

The oldest and most easterly of the islands is said to take its name from the Genoan adventurer **Lancelotti Malocello**, who in the year 1312 made for himself an outpost and a governor's mansion in the wilderness we now call Lanzarote, some 80 km from the Moroccan coast. After that episode, the history of the island is obscure until the arrival, in the year 1402, of the Norman soldiers of fortune, Juan de Bethencourt and Gadifer de la Salle, who came to claim the land for Castile, and begin the Spanish possession of the islands which continues to the present day. Episodes in that long history — viewed as though through a tinted lens — present Lanzarote as a general symptom of Europe in the rise and decline of the West.

Three Tinted Views of Lanzarote

An outpost of empire

Little white villages grow in the land, their houses
    clumped in the brow-black earth
like fungi with spores of straw; a plaintive goat
    tethered in the hot yard,
and in the fields, laborious terraces
    hoarding the vital soil
that nurtures vines and cherishes the corn.
    From coves and sheltered beaches
the boats put out, the little timeless boats,
    deft and double-ended,
with gunwale strakes of ocean blue or green,
    the sweeps poised on pintles
or maybe strops, with long blades to drive

and steer across the waves,
putting out lines for tuna, hake, sea-bass,
the ubiquitous fruta del mar
plucked for the gentry in their pleasant towns,
where soon colonial houses
raise their stone scutcheons and their patios.
The days go by and by,
each calendar a page of unevent.

Beyond horizon's grasp
two rolling centuries belong to Spain;
The ships of Spain come home
laden with silver from the Americas;
Her soldiers raise the Cross
and serve as cannon-fodder for Castile
and Christ alike; all's one,
whether Milan is occupied, or Naples
or Don John at Lepanto
stands up for Europe and the Catholic faith.
Art and letters are Spain's —
see now, Velasquez painting for King Philip,
El Greco's here, Murillo,
and writers — Lope de Vega, Calderon,
and Miguel de Cervantes,
crippled in the king's service, captured
by Barbary pirates, left
destitute in the very fame of his work,
but man immortal, blest
in the immense humanity of his laughter.

*This is a time for kings
and kingly houses with familiar claims
    on this domain or that,
this rule or that, under (of course) God.
    A Spanish king becomes
a Holy Roman Emperor; then as Habsburg
    gives place to Bourbon, Spain
loses at length the certainty of power;
    But in the islands, still
the burro hauls the burdened cart, and still
    the peasant's blackened hand
wrestles the stones in the brittle field, and still
    the inshore fisherman
tends lines, and plies the sweeps, with one eye for
    the menace of that line
where sky and wave join in a fringe of cloud.
    And in his counting-house
the merchant balances his books, and in
    the pious villages
the priest recites the changeless Mass, his hands
    fluttering over the Host.*

*For what should happen here, but life and death
    that happen everywhere?*

The Fire Mountains

*Those of us who live on a crater's rim
or on the warm slopes of a snoring hill
that may one day burst open like a door
and let the frantic demons out of school —
those of us who live with a volcano
(they are also in the heart) cannot believe
in Vulcan's imminent action. It will happen,
has happened, once, but cannot happen to us.
Signs there are, maybe; exhalations,
a whiff of sulphur in the mountain air,
a hissing fumerole, breath of the stabled beast;
The god is sporting with us; we are safe;
it cannot be in earnest. But it can.
The year is 1730. George the Second,
florid, thick spoken Hanoverian,
briefly acquainted with the English tongue,
rules in St James, and Mr Samuel Johnson
is at college in Oxford; but in Lancelot's isle
a court and college of craters speaks in tongues
of fire; mountains of fire; some twenty-eight,
erupting, solo or in chorus, over
an astonished land. The mountains rage
for six years, years of agony in which
Lancelot's isle is changed. Ten villages,
little white villages, lie choked beneath
mineral rubble, thirty feet of it.
A quarter of the island is engulfed,
and that the most fertile land; the people live
through a new conquest, a new slavery
to nature and 'needs must'; they quit the ground
their fathers worked through quiet centuries,
and nothing will ever be the same again.*

*But the poor survive the enormities of time,
outlive the inequity of heaven.. Only the rich
and the powerful die; they can afford to go.
The poor are always present, too distressed
to let their stubborn mishaps go to waste.
They must fulfill their destinies of toil,
one generation living to another
as the frail skiff shakes out its lateen sail,
as the priest mumbles over the sacred cup.
And the earth revives, the dark insulted earth
bears crops again, the corn, the pulse, the root.
They will grow onions now, the tawny globes
buried over their bellies in black beads,
the porous granules of volcanic ash.
Water is scarce — no matter, here's the trick:
each night the warm earth and cool heaven meet,
and in the exchange, a condensation fills
those cinder-crumbs with moisture. So the vines
will also grow, and stronger, so that still
the sweet wine, the malvasia, is drawn
in Lancelot's broken land. There is in this
a greater grandeur than proud palaces,
greater than regiments and cavalcades.*

*The earth survives, the earth survives, and breeds
the mute, invincible will to live and hope.*

Tenerife

The island of Tenerife is layered with the histories of occupants and economic adventure. The aboriginals, the Guanches, were self-sufficient and did not engage in commerce, but after the Spanish occupation in the 15th century, one enterprise followed another, and faltered. First sugar cane was tried, and failed; then viticulture, successful enough (as it still is) until a disastrous eruption of El Teide put paid to the wine exporting business. Later came an unlikely episode of island profit as an exporter of cochineal, derived from beetles feeding on the Prickly Pear, a cactus introduced from Mexico. With the development of chemical dyes, that, too, failed, but by then the banana was established as a cash crop. Now, though, the Canarian banana is in danger, from the competition of the American(Venezuelan) industry, and worse from the encroachments of the tourist trade, which requires land for the building of hotels, resorts, leisure complexes. The 'developers' pay handsomely, more and more farmers sell willingly. It is much easier to thrive on stock options than on growing bananas. International capital is swallowing Tenerife.

A Fallen Empire

After the sugar cane had failed, and after
his godship, the great Fire-Mountain, flung
those tides of furious mud down through the vines,
cancelling the malmsey and engulfing
the seaport, Garachico, metres deep,
there came from Mexico this cactus called
Opuntia — or else the Prickly Pear,

*for pears of a sort it yields; but not for that
the peasant set it in the uplands of the wastes
of Tenerife, those holdings in the hills
where livelihood is wrested from a soil
more grateful to the cactus than the vine.
Opuntia plays host to a weird guest,
the beetle, cochinella; cochineal's
the dye, the deep red dye that coloured once
my master's waistcoat or my dame's brocade,
and now, maybe, your lipstick or your sweets.
How strange to think that once upon a time
a world of shows, a theatre of pomps
depended on this little knave; the beetle
munching away, filling his beetle maw
with feasts of fleshy cactus, to supply
the presences of princes, pride of prelates,
the mummeries of magistrates and schools.
But nothing lasts. Opuntia's empire sank;
the dyer found another chemistry;
the aniline prevailed. So farewell, bug.
No matter; came the hour, came the banana,
now sovereign everywhere; yet even that
must yield in time; will yield to white hotels,
the new bloom of the islands, the cash crop
for sale to tourists, stacked ten stories high,
fast eating up the land the farmer tilled.*

Tomorrow — hail the Empire of Cement.

Tenerife

Ocean harangues rocks:
records of that conference
are available now in racks
of polychromatic postcards

showing a mountain, a god
feared once, for fiery excess;
" now " says the tourist guide,
" a feature not to be missed."

Note the palms, the hibiscus,
the luxuriating bars.
Music invites; a circus
of loudly abandoned balance

offers a good time, stranger;
but nothing can quite delete
the rasp of the sea in anger,
or volcano's gaunt silence.

El Teide, Tenerife

El Hierro

For centuries, until 1884, the island of Hierro, outermost of the Canarian group, was assumed to mark the prime meridian of longitude. The venturers, during the years of Spanish ascendancy, came this way to pick up a bearing on their voyage out to the fabled Americas. This was my first visit there, in one of the boxy, piston-driven skyvans that used to be operated by a local airline, Binter Canarias. My fellow passengers were workers going home for the New Year holiday. For me the journey had overtones of a more spiritual sort.

Landing Hard
(on El Hierro, Dec. 27th 1998)

Between strict hill and daft Atlantic
the little airstrip lies.
God willing, we may light upon it —
forgive us our trespasses —

(why do I make these absurd journeys,
forever blundering on,
fearful, bowed in heart, getting frailer,
nearing the end of my span ?)—

telling your beads, or humming 'Crimond',
    whether it's 'Hail Mary', or
'The Lord's my Shepherd', petition withers
    in the engine's aetheistic roar—

slam! And we're down and madly running,
    The placid **horreños** *laugh;*
they have the knack of happy landings,
    theirs is an innocent life.

But I am afraid of other islands
    that trouble the backward seas;
from shores of desire, and guilt, and failure,
    the cry to repent pursues,
murmuring still when the plane has landed
    between the surf and the slope,
and we fetch our baggage, and find a taxi,
    and get to our lodging and sleep.

El Hierro Travelogue

On New Year's Eve 1998. We hired a taxi, and the driver was our guide on a tour of the island. *'Isla de Contrastos'* he called it, **Island of Contrasts**. His pride in it was immense and proprietorial. He had been a seaman, had seen the world, but had chosen, like so many other emigrant herreños, to return to the simplicity and enchantment of his native place.

                *   *   *

El Golfo

Boot shaped! Banal the fact, the figure strange;
the instep-curve's a cruel mountain range,
the south wall of a crater: all the rest
ocean ingested, leaving this curved crest
of jagged peaks round the enchanted bight
they call El Golfo, where the capricious light
shifts between dim and dazzle, as the sky
stoops low to the Atlantic, or stands high.
At the gulf's northern headland, hunched offshore,
those hayrick-mounds, the Roques de Salmor,
were till of late the home of lizards — crude
primeval, coalmine black, a giant brood;
then southaway, at the bay's farther end,
Pozo de la Salud, a well, to mend
with waters from the sulphurous underground,
pains of the sick and tantrums of the sound.
Here flights of fancy hover, taking wing
from serpent-guarded rock to sacred spring.

Isla de Tranquilidad

*'Isle of Tranquility' the guide books call
this heaving rampart. Tranquil ? Not at all.
Watchful, maybe. Silent, immensely so,
but tranquil in the brochure's meaning ? No.
Closer inspection mocks the publicist.
A crust of magma, crumpled in the fist
of ocean ? Or an angry mouth agape
to swallow it ? Here shapes of every shape
meld into other shapes, and everywhere
are twisted outside-in — the juniper
(the island's badge) bent double in the gales,
long ropes of lava writhing like the tails
of frozen serpents—all the evidence
proclaims an unremitting turbulence
that rocks the sight and rummages the mind.
Not tranquil. Call the place, if you're inclined
to name the island from a tourist's view,
'The Island of Mutations'. That might do.*

Las Montañetas

We tourists chase the weather's changes. Cloud
visits the north, to drape a ragged shroud
of rain on flinty fields, abandoned, cold;
where drystone walls make barriers to hold
the ground in pens of pasture, or divide
neighbour from neighbour on the dank hillside.
Las Montañetas, like sweet Auburn, sprawls
deserted; broken roof and crumbling walls
all that denote a place where heretofore
stood dwellings, office, church, a village store,
the apparatus of community.
No token, this, of man's iniquity;
no greedy landlord forced a clearance; no
calamity of war laid the place low.
In these bleak moors sufficiently persist
the scourge of rain, calamity of mist —
sufficiently, to harry life, until
the heart is broken, and the labouring will.

Hoya del Morcillo

*South to the pinewoods, then, where overhead
green awnings float, and underneath is spread
the forest-carpet, gleaming russet-brown.
Still from Malpaso's reef the sky rolls down,
in sleek, fat-cat, chinchilla-white cloud-smoke,
towards the parkland where vacation folk
play pitch-and-putt, or stroll among the trees,
or sit at picnic tables, by degrees
of confidence improving every hour
that shines between a drizzle and a shower.*

*But still you seek the sun ? We'll move again
to find an Africa ensconced in Spain.*

La Restinga

Down to the boot-heel, now, our road shall run,
where La Restinga bakes in endless sun,
a breeze-block township, not as old as time,
but innocent of constables and crime.
A mole(unsightly) guards the fishing fleet
in safe, calm water; one white-coated street
confronts this harbour, dazzling the day;
swimmers dog-paddle in a blacksand bay.
A polyglot resort, but newly-grown,
where nut-brown Germans nag the public phone
in pea-green accents, and the Catalan
knows where the fish jump straight into the pan.
A bowl of limpet soup ? A tasty eel ?
A slice of octopus ? If you've a feel
for calamares, or for cuttlefish,
tuck in your napkin, friend, and name your dish.
But as for me, alas, I have no taste
for such: those ocean-juices go to waste
on my sad palate. No, believe me, sirs,
Poseidon's ugly, oily customers
have no appeal for me. Allow me, please,
my lunch of fresh bread, olives, and white cheese.

Mirador de Isora

Now to your map. This coast's accounted El
Mar de las Calmas, *and the name sits well.*
Go back uphill towards Isora: there
the mirador gives ' time to stand and stare'.
' The Sea of Calms' — rarely such calm, complete
colourbox blue as this. The noontide heat
lies on it dreamily, the narrow shore
swings down to hazed Orchilla, where, before
Greenwich's grasp on longitude began,
the lighthouse marked the prime meridian.

Here Spanish venturers came sailing home
from the Americas and Kingdom come,
and hailed (as token of accomplished luck)
the ***Roque de Bonanza*** *— 'Fortune's Rock' —*
a sculptured accident, which some declare
in shape a lizard. Others think, a bear;
'tis very like a whale; or like a wall
with door pierced through; or (frankly) like them all.

It is the warmth, perhaps, addles the sight;
the air a tenuity, the dizzy height,
a lunchtime feast of more than cheese and bread,
breed strange illusions in this veteran's head,
who gazes into timelessness, and sees
ships and their lawful-lawless purposes,
fancies the end of every voyage made —
warfare, or slavery, or simple trade,
carrack of Portugal, or Arab dhow
sees, or a British seventy-four — and now,
mazed in the glamoured silence of this coast,

dreams of a bold and many-weathered ghost,
commander of a vineleaf-green caique,
laughing and bawling at his crew — in Greek.

Dreamer, draw from the edge. We'll watch no more
from vantage point, or mind's own mirador
of miracle and mirage. We have to go
where facts are facts, and consequently know
the need to keep the earth beneath our feet.
Pack up your camera. Cover your retreat
with cliché: "Marvellous! The day's complete!"
Turn, then turn back to snatch a brief reprieve.
Click. The eye shutters. Click. We have to leave.

And so

"And so we say farewell...." Our travelogue
trots its iambics like a faithful dog,
pleased to be pleased wherever master leads,
uphill or down. This skipping style succeeds
as snapshots capture moments gone astray —
notes on experience, scribblings that say
"Do you remember ?" or "The light was bad",
"Who's this ?" and "What a lovely time we had".
But vision, seeing 'steadily and whole',
does not march with Minolta. It's the soul
that makes the seeing, the enduring light
matching the outward and the inward sight.

Blest be the power that sees beyond the sense,
through the gross tokens of experience
seeking the patterns that articulate
soul within senses — words, and the Word's inmate.
Mind frames its latent myths, as to and fro
we plot and patch our visions. On Hierro
the rain, the cloud, the sun, the violently
twisted, fire-rosy earth, the mother-sea,
the grotesque lava-fields, the guardsman pine
and hunchback juniper, construct a sign
of many signs; scope of the mind that brings
God into view, and loses worldly things.
Was it for this we came ? This brought us here
to celebrate the epiphany of the year ?
Soul will remember, poetry may tell
where soul has been. And so we say farewell....

*   *   *   *

Flower Pieces

The extraordinary wealth of ornamental plants and shrubs in the gardens and public places of Tenerife is the legacy of the late 18th century, when the Marques de Villanueva y Prado, at the command of the Spanish king Charles II, established in Puerto de la Cruz a garden of acclimatisation for exotic plants imported from all over the world. The exotics have become daily familiars. *Strelitzia* is from the Transkei, *Malvaviscus* an incomer from Mexico. Such plants and flowers become personal acquaintances — and readily take on the attributes of personality.

A Career Model
(Strelitzia Reginae)

Mademoiselle Regardez-moi, the florists' patroness,
seen to advantage in the foyers of fairly grand hotels,
among people very loosely classifiable as *nice,*
presents her profile and ignores the nasal trills
of "Strelitzia! ah Strelitzia! My favourite!"
She is everyone's favourite. Elegant—*soigné*
you would certainly have to call her, though not quite
vierge. Her accent, I would judge, a transformed Cockney.
Perfect her *maquillage,* accenting just
the right catwalk pose of averted, beaky hauteur,
and her *coiffure* strikes a balance between a joy and a jest.
She models from time to time for superior posters
or an airline's in-flight magazine, and is busy, *très
très* busy with her career; and yet, poor soul,
might justifiably complain to the artificial trees:
" *Je suis toute seule*, you know dahlings. I mean, *toute seule.*"

The Bonniest Bush
(Malvaviscus penduliflora)

*The heavenly Malvaviscus' lacquered sheen
is an intensity of lustrous red
in a prolixity of lucent green.
The bonniest bush, I think; and -be it said-
no reason palpable, no forced excuse
propels a simple partiality,
no kitchen purpose or medicinal use,
as, to relieve a clouding of the eye
or ease the turmoil of the heart. It stands
on its own careless merits; it commands
attention first, assent to Scripture next,
and in particular the Saviour's text
which says, "And therefore be ye perfect, even
as God your Father, perfect in His heaven."*

The Bougainvillea Lunch
(Bougainvillea glabra. Tulipero africano)

"Queso manchego," the waiter said, his eyes
fixed on the end of some abstruse proposition.
"And some bread," I said, " and butter, if you would,
and a 7-up, and a beer. Small." "Small," he said
as if the word were almost too small to see.
Outside the taberna we sat under an arbour
tented with bourgainvillea, a winter's day
in La Palma, at Los Llanos de Aridane,
where winter is a paradigm of May;
lay figures in a notion of Matisse,
accessories to colour, not its agents,
in the Plaza de España, taking lunch.
When it began to rain, a slow, reflective,
affable sort of rain, we wouldn't go in
as the waiter asked, his gaze coldly averted
from the cheese and the 7-up. Not every day
does one lunch in pavilions of bougainvillea. Rain
fell tactfully into our cups, one drop at a time,
and we paid our bill, and our respects to the Virgin,
whose Church of the Remedies lies at hand in the plaza,
and walked to the bus-stop, down a long street, lined
with ranks of tulip trees, an honour guard
all tricked in plumes and puggarees of red,
to march us out of town with mute hosannas.
Manchego and tulip trees, hard cheese and heaven
one winter's day on the island of La Palma,
and small beer under the spreading bougainvillea.

Loose change; keep it to pay the ferryman.

Bougainvillea

Masca

Seacliff Bougainvillea

Incomers, 2000 AD

The haunted fleets, the grey-green petrified navies
 Poseidon made
go sailing on in this archipelago
 of crumpled hulls,
motioning, motionless, endlessly swung to the south
 and beckoning west,
the old course, the course the voyagers took.

Look now, little Hierro
sails there en vedette, leading La Palma, Gomera
then Tenerife,
wearing the white trysail called Teide (glimpsed
from fifty miles out),
with Grand Canary abeam, then Fuerteventura, and so,
wallowing astern,
the first and misfortuned last of the Fortunate Isles,
sad Lanzarote.

But these are more tranquil times in Lancelot's island:
the demon's contained,
and the wreckage wrought by those ancient engines of wrath
is turned to account.
New venturers come oversea, and are ready to pay
for a footing here.
The tourist is toted on camelback up the long curve
of Timanfaya,
the rose-red, ash-grey flank of the slumbering firehill,
and waiters who serve
in the restaurant on the edge of the National Park
amuse the diners
with thrusting wisps of brushwood into a crevice
(it bursts into flame)
or grilling fish over an open well
(done in a trice)
or pouring water into a length of pipe
thrust in the ground
and fleeing the instant gout of angry steam.
Laughter, applause
declares a danger passed, a god suppressed.

       in Agadir,
close by, on the African coast, the fists of money
       rub thumb and finger.
In Cabo Verde mouths in impassive faces
       shape to a sum;
there is a charge for bringing to these islands,
       in rusted ships,
or else in rotten keels braving the current,
       the immuigrants,
wretched, lawless, dumped on some quiet beach
       — que fuerte ventura —
to wrest a living out of the burgeoning streets,
       feed on the tourist,
cheat, sell shoddy goods, evade the police.
       The eastern islands,
open for business as usual, take them in.

       Surely in time
their children will be honoured in the towns ?

Fuerteventura

The island of Fuerteventura, unspectacular and mysterious, is the second largest of the Canarian Islands. It has empty miles of golden beaches, to windward as well as to leeward, and is famed as a windsurfer's paradise. The interior is unyielding, roasting wilderness with interludes of green. The Spanish philosopher and poet, **Miguel de Unamuno** was exiled here in 1924, for having ventured to attack, in print, the dictator **Primo de Rivera**. He described his habitation, inland with a blackened crater for neighbour, as "an oasis in the desert of civilization". That does not strike one immediately; but if one were to sit still, unfretfully, the sense of it might come clear. Though his sojourn was brief (he escaped to Paris) his name and memory are honoured in the island. Primo de Rivera is hardly ever mentioned.

Little Morocco, Sahara by the sea;
it takes a flush of adspeak to describe
this wind-whipped sun-flayed island riding on
those turquoise tides that lave the shining sand.
The name comes from that rogue de Bethencourt,
a Norman, pillaging for self and Spain,
who once exclaimed (tradition tells the tale)
Que fuerte ventura! *— "What a great adventure!"*

But what could he have seen in it ? Perhaps
promise of treasure in those brooding hills,
perhaps a prefecture to call his own
(he named his capital Betancuria),
perhaps the brutal joy of subjugation,
putting the simple tribesmen to the sword
for Jesus or Castile or both at once,
baptising captives into slavery,
the piety of empire, then as ever.

Fuerte — *'strong'; well-chosen epithet,
not **buono** not **bonita**. This is not
a pretty place. There is a dearth of green;
trees are a luxury, shadow an indulgence;
the land is tawny, beautiful in that
and mainly that, corn-yellow at high noon,
russet and copper in the evening light,
the beauty of unflinching wilderness.*

*Heat and the scouring gales make history
a laughing-stock; de Bethencourt's domain
comes down to flaking plaster and peeled paint,
derelict windmills in the roasting fields,
a harsh land barely good enough for goats
(even the lizards find the living hard),
alloted to the Spanish Foreigh Legion
whose soldiery patrol the dismal streets
of new Puerto Rossario, chief town,
Puerto de Cabras once (meaning Goatport,
the name being changed to give its face a lift).*

*Now tourists come and tour. Developers
develop. Bars and trinket-shops and squads
of slot-machines invest the sad resorts.
The rubble and the rind of money fill
the promenades where backward baseball caps,
beer bellies, tee shirts, bosoms, backsides, drift
towards the consolations of the night.
The Spaniard drives a cab, or waits at table,
Africans tout cheap watches round the bar.*

*There's a despair in this, an emptiness
that shrinks the heart, a greyness on the screen
behind the eyes. Cruising for our diversions,
slowly we die; and nothing's worse for soul
than joining willy-nilly in the fun".
Fun (one of course joins in) is a yearning waste,
pretence of pleasure, uneven of joy,
a Waste that owns no kin with Wilderness.
In Wilderness is where the soul revives.
"What went ye into the wilderness to see?
A reed shaken by the wind?" — the words of Christ
echo uncomfortably here; so few of us
go into the wilderness now, to see a reed,
to see a prophet, even to see a God.
"Let me have company" the traveller prays.
"Give us our daily treat." And so we fail.*

*Miguel de Unamuno loved this place:
"In civilization's desert an oasis."
Philosopher-in-exile, resident
before the airstrip and the breezeblock age,
he saw no doubt what our estranging vision
distracts us from, that we are best at ease
when all pretence is peeled; the sun, the wind,
the stark conditions of a barren land,
can show the way to hope. A mystery*
fuerte ventura — *noble venture. Yes.
Could one but find the courage, or the time.*

*   *   *

The Eighth Island.

In the Canarian archipelago, there are seven larger islands, several islets or skerries, and a recurrent optical illusion, which, when seen from the west coast of Tenerife, is possibly the loom of the island of La Palma, away to the west and north. Tenerifeans call this phantom San Borondón; reports go back to the 18th century and earlier.

The eighth island, shadow-resort of wraiths,
though seen but seldom, may present itself
under the specious colour of mirage:
a cloud, perhaps, at the horizon's edge,
illusion maybe of the mirrored light
raising the phantom of the inverted hills
on the Canarian sea. San Borondón,

named after Brendan, that Hibernian monk
who took a ship to find the Blessed Isles
and came at last upon this vagrant shape
designed by God, lowered like scenery
into the theatre of sea and sky,
a place for sainthood to forget itself,
no staithe or staging-post for lesser folk.

Mark, though, the seaman's yarn, a likely tale:
some captain, doubtful of his longitude
(kinsman, perhaps, of Lemuel Gulliver)
comes close enough to see the smoke of dwellings,
sees woods and pastures, herds of cattle, men
tending the herds, yet cannot make the land:
logs the event, then loses it in mist.

I, too, have seen it; hull down, ominous,
a sombre landfall for the travelling eye,
on afternoons in March or late November
in dropping light, bearing Nor' West by West
across a pallid sea: San Borodŏn,
the outer edge of possibility,
shade of a shape, not marked on any chart,

but wavering in the mind's coordinates;
not reached by ferry from the tourist shore,
nor aeroplane, nor sleek white cruising ship;
whoever goes there makes the trip alone,
borne in a bone-and-leather coracle,
praying for grace to find a haven in
the last resort of self-forgetfulness..

Colophon: Tempus Edax Rerum

Tolerant only of ocean, time
Effaces only the subtle and the solid;
Music and mathematics as well as marble's
Purple effrontery and the pallid
Understatements of humble slate
Sink into that crumbling flood where

Every trace of wit and occupation
Disappears, distinction washed away;
All things on earth defer to the unending
Xenophobic rant of immense tides

Railing at the intrusions of our frail
Everyday histories; declaring our tenancy
Rootless, mocking our island rock,
Unmastered forever, except by the One and Only
Maker and Master of all, unmaking time.

The Skies

The weather of the Canaries is a charming conundrum; each island has its weathers, and there are variations of weather within each island. The predominant winds, *los Alisos*, the Trade winds are north westerlies, which seem, as the face feels them, and the sky shows them, more westerly than north. Northerly winds, cold and rainbearing, stem from anticyclonic movement round the Azores. Periodically the wind veers to the east, and becomes the *sirocco*, the dust-bearing *calima*. We read the sky and come to second guess the winds swirling about our island, but the skies change subtly, day by day, hour by hour.

Weather Wisdoms
(Tenerife, on the West Coast)

The seaside wind's a jovial westerley,
brash kiss-me-sailorboy, ruffling the lace
of swaggering waves, and blowing into port
to preen the palms and flirt among the flags;
happy, until some clash of temperaments
in mid-Atlantic brings the sailor home
in a foul mood. Up from the beach at night
he staggers, yawping fit to raise the roof,
shrills in the slats of the shutters, bounces bins
down cringing alleys, chivvies plastic chairs
round the verandah, stifles ribald cries
of homing revellers. Householders drive
wedges under the windows, jam the doors
to quell the accursed rattle, crouch in bed
nervously, longing for sleep and morning's proof
that we are here and whole and housed and not

*careering piecemeal down the **avenida**.*

*How can this last ? How long, O Lord, how long ?
"Three days," the locals say. "Three days or four,
five at the most. It never blows for long."*

*Veer a point. Shifting north, the wind becomes
delinquent in a different style; a wrecker
driving the close-hauled clouds in fat flotillas
to founder on the cliffs and mountain-reefs
of our rock-lofty island; bringing rain
to green the north, sweet spill of rain to fill
the earth below the earth, the aquifers,
the little resevoirs that farmers make
to feed their famished terraces. And thus
the rain falls, on the just and unjust, too.
On folk assignable to neither class
it freely falls; on the streetside café
falls, where the tables weep; on the **pastelería**
falls, and the hotel tennis courts. A flood
dances downstairs by the Church of the Holy Spirit,
turning our plaza, where the roller-bladers
romp, after school, in reckless figurations,
into a rink of raddled water, crossed
with care by ageing folk with porous bones.*

*How can this last ? How long, O Lord, how long ?
"Three days," the locals say. "Three days or four,
five at the most. It never lasts for long."*

The landside wind's a lout called the **calima**
sibling to the **sirocco,** *bred in the Atlas,*
migrating to these islands, where it spreads
wanhope and atheism and sullen spite.
The loping dervish-wind that sets the teeth
to grind on dust, red dust, that ferries flies
to feast on slumbrous faces, makes the eyes
burn in the dry blast, and the windpipe rasp,
is, some might say, the devil's calling card.
Children fall ill when the **calima** *blows,*
and adults suffer humours of the soul.
Post office clerks have fantasies of tossing
sacks full of mail down elevator shafts,
and pretty shopgirls harbour glitternig thoughts
of strangling awkward madams, their sweet mouths
taut in a brilliant rictus of ill will.
Good friends fall out. Wives are averse to husbands.
This is his doing, the rogue, whose oven-breath
loiters in every corner of the square.

How can this last ? How long, O Lord, how long ?
"Three days," the locals say. "Three days or four,
five at the most. It never stays for long."

But sun's the normal one. Regular as
rhythm, sun gets up behind the town
and does his daily dive into the sea,
ten hours a day for seven days a week,
playing a blinder, as the sportsmen say,
and his consistency is almost boring.
Whether in bland mid-morning, or the stupor
of three in the afternoon, the sun persists,
knowing full well his business is to shine,

*and not without a touch of showmanship,
he shines at it; the spangles on the ocean,
the underpainting of the evening sky,
effects devised by sun for our delight,
become, at length, delightful commonplace.
Sun help us, we grow weary of the sun,
or so obtusely languid that we feel
a little downpour might not come amiss.*

*How can this last ? How long, O Lord, how long ?
"Three months," the locals say. "Three months or four,
five at the most. It breaks before too long."*

*Traveller, there's morality in this,
to take or leave alone, as the spirit moves.
Read in these weathers of an island coast —
where we sit down to meditate at length
on the finality of ocean —read,
as you may choose, the emblems of a time,
perhaps your time: adversities, corruptions,
the long oblivion of the ordinary —
or else read nothing in it, only let
wind blow, rain fall, sun shine as usual,
without regard to faith, or prophecy.
No sense in dwelling on it, you may think.*

*(Yet still you seek a sense beyond the senses
unceasingly, and all things speak of it.).....*

* * * *

Easter in the Pueblo

You who this day arose
out of the cave's stale murk—the story goes—
and leaving tell-tale on the ground
your shroud and cerements unwound,
ascended to the white
kingdom of everlasting light,

bless my dark unbelief,
my spirit masterless, my uninstructed heart
that will not lift
out of its cleft of clay, or make a shift
to grow away from grief,
or, fearing greatly, set its fears apart;

and if I have no hope to rise
into that everlasting paradise
pledged with your ancient gift of wine and bread,
let a brief earthen jubilee be mine,
this tipsy festival that turns my head—
the clustering prattle of the flame vine,

hibiscus trumpeting, the glow
of bougainvillea like a purple snow,
bright oleander's brag; but most of all,
and truest to this time, the plangent fall
of the jacaranda, violet blue,
heavenly blue, Sir, as your mother's shawl.

Such wantonness may bring me near to you.

* * *

But there are always fiestas to cheer us: they supply the

calendar with public holidays and time-outs, whether in the *romerías* days devoted to the numerous local saints, or in the major religious feasts, like Corpus Christi, or the prolonged secular jollities of the yearly *Carnaval*.

A popular event is the *Cabalgata de los Tres Reyes Magos* (Cavalcade of the Three Wise Kings) when the Magi ride into town (or in some coastal places arrive by boat) bearing gifts for the children, by pre-arrangement with indulgent parents.

A play of the Epiphany is performed, usually by schoolchildren. In some places the scripts are traditional, and of some age; mostly the scenarios are devised by the teachers who rehearse the young performers. Often the Christ-child is a doll, suitably swaddled, nursed with tenderness and solicitude by a ten-year old Mary; but at the first performance I saw, the heavenly babe had a human representative, four months old.

Epiphany in the Pueblo

*In a quiet corner of the village where the
main road swerves past the general store
one of the Three Wise Men is puffing a
cigarette and the others are adjusting their
tinsel crowns and cotton wool beards and
splendidly theatrical swathes of superannuated
bedcovering as they wait for the horses to
come and take them into our Bethlehem and
the papier-maché* **posada** *over which a huge
star has emphatically stopped —*
Vivan los Tres Reyes Magos! Vivan!

*for our neighbourhood artist has created a
backdrop with the star zooming in like a
Captain Marvel space-rocket and to confirm
the message a road sign reading To the Inn
leads the eye unerringly to the stage where
local children are to enact the good old
story under the professional eye of our
announcer and* **maestra de ceremonias**
who warms up the crowd with cries of
Vivan los Tres Reyes Magos! Vivan!

*while children totter about in rehearsed
impulses of adoration and Joseph the
gangliest kid on the block stands flapping
his hands distressfully at the crib as if to
say this is none of my doing which we
know full well it isn't because this year's
Sacred Infant by special arrangement with
the organising committee is little Roberto
Gonzales not four months old yet and
sleeping good as gold, bless him —*
Vivan los Tres Reyes Magos! Vivan!

as Maria-Luz and Ana and Conchita and Jaime
and Fernando and Pablo and all the glorious
company of heaven in wired haloes and ditto
wings give squeaky voice to their amazement
and harmonising in slightly acidulous thirds
sing of the beauty of this night while the
maestra reads aloud the imperishable story
of those who followed the star and found
first the villainous Herod and then the
Christ-child in a manger lying —
Vivan los Tres Reyes Magos! Vivan!

at which even my sceptical septuagenarian
knees might well bend with a crack like a
popgun so simple the tale and so tender but
I sit on my balcony cradling my one
permitted glass of red wine musing and
smiling while the **maestra** periodically
breaks off her recital to explain like a
railway announcer that due to unforeseen
circumstances such as the non-appearance
of suitable mounts the arrival of the
Wise Men will be delayed and no wonder
for this is Spain where even history
rarely happens on time —
Vivan los Tres Reyes Magos! Vivan!

*till at last a stir in the crowd tells us that
they are now on their way having made
the trip from the furthermost bounds of
the Orient and into view they come uneasily
perched on their slow and remarkably
continent nags (camels would never have
done) and ride to the plaza a journey of
all of a hundred yards before dismounting
and processing to the stage where after they
have paid their respects to Roberto Gonzalez
locum tenens to the Messiah they sit in
all their bearded majesty and mystery on
three gold-painted kitchen chairs to preside
over the night's principal business which is
as ever the distribution of gifts —*
Vivan los Tres Reyes Magos! Vivan!

*but it being now long past the bedtimes of
the intended recipients of the gifts the
maestra is obliged to read out several times
(with tetchy threats of non-delivery should
the addressees not come forward this instant
to claim the football or fairy cycle or home
doctor kit or roller skates or battery-powered
model car or Barbie doll or annihilator space
ray-gun or other largesse of the remarkably
wised-up Wise Men) the names of children
who eventually wake for long enough to mount
the stage and having braved the beards for a
bushy kiss receive their presents after which
they weave around like little drunks until
their mothers come to fetch them down —*
Vivan los Tres Reyes Magos! Vivan!

*and at length the tale is told and the
youngsters are abed and the Wise Men have
disrobed and unbearded and gone for a
couple of drinks before turning in and the
plaza is a squalid mess of streamers and
wrapping paper and cola cans, and still,
so still, I sit on my balcony looking west
into the night sky where Venus has risen
bright and lonely, and I think one star
will do as well as another if one is trusting
like a child, or wise like a diligent seeker
who has sought long and patiently and
at last found an answer. And I smile a little
at the echo, sharp and wistful, in my head —*
Vivan los Tres Reyes Magos! Vivan!

The Patroness of Tenerife

In this Catholic country devotion to the Blessed Virgin is commonplace and passionate. She is the object of reverence and pilgrimage. The Patroness of Tenerife is the **Virgin of Candelaria**, venerated in legend for her miraculous powers. In the island of San Miguel de la Palma, *Nuestra Señora de las Nieves* is revered in her chapel in the hills under the snowline, from which she is brought down every year to the capital, to preside over her fiesta, and every fifth year to a special festival, *La Bajada de la Virgen*, the 'Descent of the Virgin'. She is tiny, gorgeously robed, and sits amid a wealth of gold and silver from the Americas. No one visiting her shrine could doubt the total devotion of the *palmeros*. Canarians take their religion joyously— and in utter earnest. In the presence of such a devotion, strenuous and easy, the outsider feels pathos and delight and envy.

Nuestra Señora de las Nieves
(La Palma)

San Miguel de la Palma is her home.
She keeps a hacienda in the hills
where guardian ranks of laurel trees, and groves
of oranges and lemons hedge about
her simple stone-faced chapel; and within,
a plummy silence, bloomed and fragrant, breathes
the stillness of Our Lady of the Snows.

So small; a doll with terra-cotta face,
gorgeously sheened in furs and broidered silks,
she sits high in her chancel, throned above
a ziggurat of silver and wrought gold,
and looks with blank benignity upon
the shuffling pilgrims who come here to light
a candle for Our Lady of the Snows,

Lodged in her folded arm, but crazily,
a doll's doll, tucked in like an afterthought,
the Christ-child leans; her sceptre, in effect,
the badge and token of her errand here;
that tilted baton with its finial crown
the sign and warrant of her work of grace,
her office as Our Lady of the Snows,

which is to intercede for all who bring
the burden of their hearts, in true belief;
and when I think of that, I turn away,
and quit the shrine, and walk outside, and stare
at the quicksilver brilliance of the sea.
Maybe she cannot intercede for me,
this gentle, dapper, Lady of the Snows.

New Year

New Year is celebrated in the Canaries —at least in the island capitals —in much the same style as in the rest of Spain: with pleasant drifting and promenading, and neighbourly jostling, and dancing, and drinking without inhibition, and waiting for midnight when, at each of the twelve strokes of the town clock, a grape must be swallowed; and then the gloriously extravagant fireworks, and a feeling of having in some way, in some elusive sense, survived and arrived.

Another New Year
(S:ta Cruz de la Palma,1999)

The promenade is thronged,
the cobbled alleys thrum
with an oddly civil sort
of pandemonium.

Last year, as good as gone,
lingers to kiss the next;
the Town Hall clock prepares
to speak its ponderous text.

Fireworks, leaping up
from their nook beside the bay,
yell "Hi !" to America
three thousand miles away.

*Then earnestly the young
address the joyous night;
Pepita sulks; Miguel
and Ana pick a fight,*

*and on a flight of steps,
wearing his Sunday best
(ready for morning Mass)
Paco sinks down to rest—*

*who, at the summoning bell
will rise, immaculate,
and steer a course for church
approximately straight.*

*I, rooming at the inn,
salute the infant year
with toast and orange juice,
And think, "Well,—we are here."*

Canarian Hours

*One might almost think
when the sky is swept and scored with white,
feathery upward-lifting wisps of light,
might think—might almost think—gazing at those
squadrons of mistiness on the morning air,
might wish, I suppose—might very nearly suppose
      that angels were there..*

*You could almost swear
when the sea hurls in, among crinkled rocks
crashing, to sling up dazzling shocks of spume,
could swear —almost — behind that veil,
that rage of lofted silk, that rainbow-storm,
appears, with trembling arms up-fling, a pale
      prophetic form.*

*I can well believe
when the sun at noon glaring precisely down,
reducing every shadow in the town
to a wedge of black, leaches colour away
from gaudy things, laving petal and bract
with a milky sheen— I can believe this day
      a miraculous act.*

*and I will confess
in the calm honeylight of eventide
when the folded sea unscrolls by the pleated side
of a basalt cliff, and bathers leave the beach
with the gathering of the breeze and the shift of shade
across the sand, I will confess that each
      hour is God-made.*

*So must affirm
at vespers, when black ledges of the sky
glow with the crimson light of sanctuary,
the slanting rays beneath striking like swords,
streamers of delicate green floating above—
so must declare the earth to be the Lord's
and the fulness thereof.*

Mañana

Mañana *rules the islands, under (indeed) God.*
Mañana, mañana pasado
(that's the day after **mañana**), *the flowers nod*
busily, the waves of ocean break
lustily, the breezes have palms to shake,
and the barmen are always **si, muy ocupado.**

Mañana, por la mañana, *the promised plumber may come,*
or duly fail to appear;
God willing (indeed) he plumbs or declines to plumb,
and the toilet suite he ordered from Spain
is adrift in **Mañana**— *if ordered again*
Mañana *could be in January next year.*

Men might weary of this, and women even more,
who love to get things done,
but the yoke of **Mañana** *grows easier to endure*
as the sleepy syllables invest the name,
Mañana, *with an acceptable shame.*
It is sweet to shrug, and turn one's face to the sun.

" Tomorrow and tomorrow and tomorrow " someone said—
but that's our British way,
creeping from hope to hope until hope is dead.
Canarian **Mañana** *never creeps,*
Mañana's *the time the laid-back sunset keeps.*
Mañana *is yesterday asleep in today.*

Entre Chien et Loup
(Twilight 28° N 17° W)

Between a daylight and a dark,
between a visor and a veil,
evening begins;
so cool the air, so sweet,
jewels of lamplight glint between
the velvet pauses of the street —
diamond, ambe, tourmaline,

and for an hour the world is held
floating upon a languid state
of timeless calm;
nothing will happen here
until a sea breeze breaks the spell,
and music starts, and crowds appear
for shopping, strolling, dining well,

and so the neon signs will blaze
and fill the plaza with a crude
semblance of life,
a parody of light,
but at the edges of the town
true darkness brings the enormous night
silent, mocking, glittering down.

Morena Salada

Canarian girls take the eye, and the heart, with their natural elegance, their graceful carriage, their evident and unaffected enjoyment of life. But carefree youth is short. My **morena salada,** "bonny brunette" was a shopgirl, perhaps 17 years old, a year or so away from marriage and family and a long contention with the sunlight that gives and relentlessly takes; that nourishes the spirit and year by year destroys the physical bloom. From my seat at a café table I watched her crossing the town square, complete and confident in her flirtateous self-awareness, and was seized at once with affection and melancholy.

You, Señorita Legs, Miss Gloryhead,
proud-maned and comely as a thoroughbred;
watching you caracole across the square,
slantwise, half-turned to see who sees you there,
knowing I know you see me; as you go
a love-song long since lost comes home to me:

> **yo de amor me muero**
> **desde que te vi,**
> **morena salada,**
> **desde que te vi**

Dear Lass, it's not the tedious lust of flesh
(God and long-since have freed me from that mesh—
let others seek the net, I do not move),
not that which makes me sing, "I die for love
since first I saw you, brown enchantress." No,
it is for beauty's wistful brevity

> *yo de amor me muero*
> *desde que te vi,*
> *morena salada,*
> *desde que te vi.*

The flower I hold gives off the pungent smell,
fugitive savour of the marguerite —
so quick the charm, the zest too soon dispelled —
a petal plucked, between my fingers held,
crushed — and the poignant moment falters; so
inconstant is the scent, so constantly

> *yo de amor me muero*
> *desde que te vi,*
> *morena salada,*
> *desde que te vi.*

All that is marked for sprightliness and death,
as sparks flung from the fire's sunken core
glister the dark a second, and no more;
for this, because of this, because I know
the passion of a grave frivolity,

> *yo de amor muero*
> *desde que te vi,*
> *morena salada,*
> *desde que te vi.*

A Nocturne for Atlantis

(There is a legend, one of many such, that the lost city of Atlantis lies in the deep sound between the Canarian islands of Tenerife and Gomera)

en gång, ja en gång för oss ock
slocknandets kommande timme ar satt

one day, yes, one day for us, too,
extinction's advancing moment is fixed.
        — Gustav Frödling, *Atlantis*

Three hundred metres from the voluble town
enter the cool uncomplicated night;
the moon's untainted radiance floods the heaven.
Be still; a light air flirts among the palms,
the waves come loping in from Florida
to growl and snuffle round the basalt cliffs.
The sea's a crumpled cloth, blue-black, white-fringed,
with knots and threads of gold, here in the sound
between two islands. And it's here, some say,
sunken Atlantis lies; and here, they say,
were the Hesperides, the Fortunate Isles,
a garden-state of earthly happiness.
They say, they say; legends old karaoke.

Well — what if it were true, what if Atlantis
really were there, under the fidgeting sea ?
Could moon let down drift-nets of wavering light
through the dark water — what might they enmesh ?
Bonito bustling in the agora ? Cephalopods
lunched in the atrium of some ruined villa ?
Bottle-nosed whales in deep debate ? Dolphins
in the palaestra, sporting ?

*Andrew Marvell
(who never came to Atlantis — Hull was enough)
thought ocean held the icons of the land.
"Each kind doth straight its own resemblance find",
he said. A precept there for politics:
at home, in our great Mother-Parliament,
we've seen the kindred of the Moray eel;
old turtles cruising in the House of Peers;
slick party squids, emitting jets of ink;
jesting shark-mouths. But Marvell seriously
proposed his vision as a fact of science.
For us all facts dissolve in fantasies.*

*The moon, fantasy-maker, strolls aloft.
Science has unheavened her somewhat; we know
perhaps more than we care to know about
that huge mineral fragment, quondam goddess
hung in the sky, pegged to the pull of the Earth —
yet how we fancy her, Selene; this
discredited, demythologised hunk of rock
can still incite the heart to grief or glory
or sweet acceptance of necessity.*

*Our childhood's moon was nursery rhyme and mischief —
smugglers, highwaymen, that "ghostly galleon
 tossed upon cloudy seas" we memorised
for classroom recitation; or the face
 of something almost human in the sky,
watching us in a kindly, mimic way,
her space a theatre for our designs,
a crony, counsellor, or family friend.*

*"The moon hath raised her lamp above", my father
sang, at the piano; we sang with him,
mimicking harmonics and dotted rhythms,
he laughing at our juvenile inventions,
"To light the way to thee, my love,
To thee, my love, to thee, my love" —
before love was a word to conjure with.*

*"To thee, my love", I say, remembering
that sailing, wartime moon, young sweetheart's moon;
the streets, silent; brisk, winter-scent of frost
and the girl's arm in mine, her hand in mine —
her warm, bare hand! O glory in the air,
the heart's virginal thrilling! (They will smile,
those weary children of experience,
the coital and narcophagic youth
of nowadays, for whom virginity,
like consciousness, is not a lot to lose).*

*We live and learn. A cautionary light
suffuses middle age; the moon's a thing
to draw the blinds against; Tom Hardy cried
"Shut out that stealing moon" — and then shut out
remembrance of whatever was, and then
reminder of whatever might have been;
and there is nothing left remarkable,
nothing but work to do and debts to pay,
short breath and clouded eye and wearying heart.
So we'll go no more a-roving; stray no more
into the cool, uncomplicated night
our childhood wondered at, our youth-time loved.*

*But then, come age, we know the moon again,
as softly she goes up the sky, and stirs
a craving in the heart; for — purity ?;
to face things as they are, to love what is,
and bless the apparent world, without the search
for symbols, theatres, interpretations.
Save us from poor pretences; let us stand
in the scrutiny of heaven, and hope for grace.*

*There's no lost city there under the sea.
Here's your Atlantis, drowning in your skull.
The tides hiss in your ears; your eyes, blinking,
revolve swift calendars of days and nights.
Darkly we see; one day we shall not see.
"One day, yes, one day for us, too,
extinction's advancing moment is fixed"—
the senses' colonnade, brain's intricate vaulting,
memory, language, poetry, calculus,
all the brave pageantry of thought, must one day
Stop.*

*Be still; suffer the night wind's gentle touch,
suffer the murmuring of the tide, suffer
the moon's calm light; rejoice in what exists,
acclaim the Earth's unreasoned loveliness,
for that remains the argument of heaven.*

*Be still; stand where Atlantis stands, and think,
tomorrow is the day you have to leave.*

* * *

Have to Leave

That *unreasoned loveliness* is the haunting power of Canary, that brings its aliens back to the islands, year by year, as tourists, as semi-residents (called *golondrinas*, swallows) until at last they resign themselves to permanent residence in this over-developed, breeze-blocked, traffic-jammed, high-hotel--crammed and still unreasoningly lovely place. Heaven's argument is at times wistful, though; the pilgrim among so much beauty can know a lyrical, lilting, painful sense of exclusion. The charm of *primavera* is a recollection of mortality.

More of Walter Nash's poems available on-line from

Gary A David
http://www.cybertrails.com/~islandhills/workstable.htm